SPIRIT LISTOGRAPHY

MY INNER SELF IN LISTS

CREATED BY LISA NOLA

ILLUSTRATIONS BY BECCA STADTLANDER

CHRONICLE BOOKS
SAN FRANCISCO

ISBN 978-1-4521-4833-5

Manufactured in China

MIX
Paper from
responsible sources
FSC™ C008047

Illustrations by Becca Stadtlander

See the full range of Listography products at www.chroniclebooks.com.

Chronicle Books publishes distinctive books and gifts. From award-winning
children's titles, bestselling cookbooks, and eclectic pop culture to acclaimed
works of art and design, stationery, and journals, we craft publishing that's
instantly recognizable for its spirit and creativity. Enjoy our publishing and
become part of our community at www.chroniclebooks.com.

10 9 8 7 6 5 4 3 2

Chronicle Books LLC
680 Second Street
San Francisco, CA 94107
www.chroniclebooks.com

THIS BOOK IS DEDICATED
TO THE YEAR 2015:
MY YEAR OF LOSS, LEARNING,
AND TRANSFORMATION

IF I WERE A SONG, I'D BE _____

IF I WERE A TREE, I'D BE _____

IF I WERE A FLOWER, I'D BE _____

IF I WERE A FILM, I'D BE _____

IF I WERE A FOOD, I'D BE _____

IF I WERE A BIRD, I'D BE _____

IF I WERE A CAR, I'D BE _____

IF I WERE A PAINTING, I'D BE _____

IF I WERE A PLACE, I'D BE _____

IF I WERE A BOOK, I'D BE _____

IF I WERE A VEGETABLE, I'D BE _____

IF I WERE A DOG, I'D BE _____

IF I WERE A _____ , I'D BE _____

CREATE YOUR OWN

A FEW WEEKS BEFORE I LOST MY MOTHER TO CANCER, I CAME UPON HER CRYING IN HER ROOM. SHE SAID TO ME, "I AM REALLY GOING TO MISS EATING A PIECE OF TOAST." THIS MOMENT HAS REMAINED WITH ME AS A GIFT FROM HER. I REGULARLY REMIND MYSELF TO APPRECIATE THE BEAUTY OF LITTLE THINGS AND TO VIEW MY TIME HERE WITH A GREATER PERSPECTIVE—WHICH IS HARD TO KEEP SIGHT OF SOMETIMES. THAT IS WHY THIS PARTICULAR BOOK IS VERY SPECIAL TO ME.

THE *LISTOGRAPHY* SERIES NURTURES OUR SENSE OF GRATITUDE AND ASKS US TO REMEMBER, TO REDEFINE, AND TO BE CREATIVE WITH OUR LIVES. *SPIRIT LISTOGRAPHY* IS HERE TO HELP US REFLECT AND FOCUS ON OUR SPIRIT AND ON LOVE. IT BORROWS LESSONS I'VE LEARNED FROM FRIENDS, FAMILY, TEACHERS, AND AUTHORS. THIS JOURNAL IS ALSO A FUN WAY TO KEEP A WATCHFUL EYE OVER OUR SOULS, WHICH ARE ULTIMATELY OUR MOST IMPORTANT WORKS OF ART.

WHAT A MYSTERY IT IS TO ALL BE HERE TOGETHER ON THIS AMAZING PLANET. WE ARE COLLECTING EXPERIENCES, BUILDING OUR CHARACTERS, AND ESTABLISHING OUR VALUES. I HOPE YOU HAVE A GOOD LIFE FILLED WITH ALL THE BEAUTIFUL ELEMENTS OF HUMAN EXPERIENCE . . . INCLUDING A NICE PIECE OF TOAST.

LISA NOLA
WWW.LISTOGRAPHY.COM

SURFING

THINGS I'D TELL AN ALIEN TO EXPERIENCE
WHILE VISITING EARTH

ASK FOR GUIDANCE WHEN I REACH
A FORK IN THE ROAD

THINGS TO INCLUDE IN MY PRAYERS OR MEDITATIONS

EQUALITY

VALUES THAT ARE MOST IMPORTANT TO ME

WILL MISS TREES BUT NOT PLASTIC BAGS

THINGS I WILL MISS AND NOT MISS
WHEN I LEAVE THE EARTH ONE DAY

MISS

NOT MISS

MY GRANDMA AND ROBIN WILLIAMS

WHOM I'D DRAFT IN HEAVEN AS MY
TEAM OF GUARDIAN ANGELS

THIS AMERICAN LIFE RADIO PROGRAMMING

POWDERED WIGS

I'M HAPPY I AM ALIVE AND I WAS NOT
ALIVE AT THE SAME TIME AS . . .

HAPPY I AM ALIVE FOR

HAPPY I WASN'T ALIVE FOR

WATCHING DOGS PLAY AT THE DOG PARK

FAVORITE WAYS TO RELAX

A HUMMINGBIRD

I WOULDN'T MIND BEING REINCARNATED INTO . . .

I'M REUNITED WITH ALL MY PETS

WHAT I WOULD LOVE THE AFTERLIFE TO BE LIKE

BETRAY A FRIEND

I PROMISE MYSELF NEVER TO . . .

WORDS TO CAPTURE WHO I AM AND WHO I AM NOT

WHO I AM   WHO I AM NOT

GOOD LISTENER WITH CUTE TOES

NICE THINGS ABOUT ME

INNER SELF

OUTER SELF

I CAN DO THAT!

NEGATIVE AND POSITIVE THOUGHTS IN MY HEAD

NEGATIVE   POSITIVE

MY BOARD GAME STRATEGIES

THINGS TO IMPROVE

MY CAT'S FUR

MY FAVORITE THINGS TO SMELL

FALL LEAVES

MY FAVORITE THINGS TO SEE

BIRDSONG

MY FAVORITE THINGS TO HEAR

FRESHLY BAKED COOKIES

MY FAVORITE THINGS TO TASTE

THE HEAT FROM A CAMPFIRE

MY FAVORITE THINGS TO TOUCH OR FEEL

AFTERNOON TEA

MY PERFECT DAY FROM BEGINNING
TO END WOULD INCLUDE . . .

ART MUSEUM VISITS

EXPERIENCE THE SILENCE OF OUTER SPACE

I WOULD LOVE TO KNOW WHAT IT FEELS LIKE TO . . .

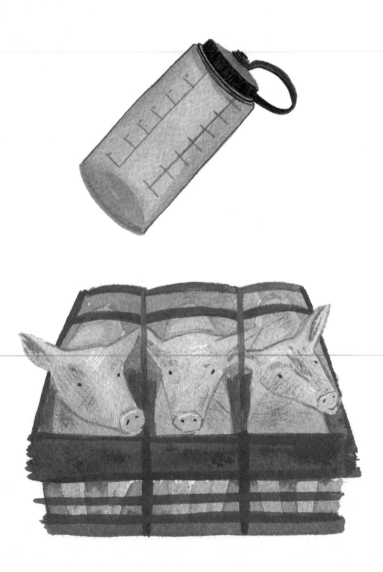

USE MY OWN WATER BOTTLE AND

RESEARCH FACTORY FARMING

WAYS TO CARE FOR THE PLANET AND LIVING THINGS

DOING

TO DO

VOLUNTEER WITH SENIOR CITIZENS

ORGANIZATIONS AND CAUSES I CARE ABOUT

VOLUNTEERED / DONATED / MARCHED FOR

_____ V D M

_____ V D M

_____ V D M

_____ V D M

_____ V D M

_____ V D M

_____ V D M

_____ V D M

_____ V D M

_____ V D M

_____ V D M

_____ V D M

_____ V D M

_____ V D M

_____ V D M

_____ V D M

_____ V D M

_____ V D M

_____ V D M

TO VOLUNTEER / DONATE / MARCH FOR

_____ V D M

_____ V D M

_____ V D M

_____ V D M

_____ V D M

_____ V D M

_____ V D M

_____ V D M

_____ V D M

_____ V D M

_____ V D M

_____ V D M

_____ V D M

_____ V D M

_____ V D M

_____ V D M

_____ V D M

_____ V D M

_____ V D M

COMPANIES TO SUPPORT AND TO BOYCOTT

TO SUPPORT

TO BOYCOTT

BRING CANNED GOODS
TO A FOOD BANK

MAKE A DONATION IN
HONOR OF A FRIEND

LEAVE A
SURPRISE BIG TIP

BUILD A PLAYGROUND FOR A
NEIGHBORHOOD IN NEED

GOOD DEEDS

COMPLETED   TO DO

------------------------------   □   ------------------------------
------------------------------   □   ------------------------------
------------------------------   □   ------------------------------
------------------------------   □   ------------------------------
------------------------------   □   ------------------------------
------------------------------   □   ------------------------------
------------------------------   □   ------------------------------
------------------------------   □   ------------------------------
------------------------------   □   ------------------------------
------------------------------   □   ------------------------------
------------------------------   □   ------------------------------
------------------------------   □   ------------------------------
------------------------------   □   ------------------------------
------------------------------   □   ------------------------------
------------------------------   □   ------------------------------
------------------------------   □   ------------------------------
------------------------------   □   ------------------------------
------------------------------   □   ------------------------------
------------------------------   □   ------------------------------

CLEAN WATER FOR ALL

WISHES FOR THE WORLD

HONESTY

QUALITIES I SEEK IN A COMPANION

MY HIGH SCHOOL DRAMA TEACHER

NURTURING RELATIONSHIPS I'VE
HAD THROUGHOUT MY LIFE

TRISHA'S HUMILITY

QUALITIES I ADMIRE IN THE PEOPLE I KNOW

PERSON | QUALITY I ADMIRE

BEING DIFFERENT IS WAY COOLER THAN BEING THE SAME

WHAT I WOULD TELL MY TEENAGE SELF

IT'S NEVER TOO LATE!

WHAT I WOULD TELL MY SENIOR-CITIZEN SELF

PLACING FRESH FLOWERS IN A VASE

LITTLE THINGS I LOVE IN LIFE

GRIFFITH PARK

INSPIRING PARKS AND NATURE HIKES

FAVORITES

TO DO

WILD HORSES

MEMORABLE THINGS I'VE WITNESSED

DRIVING

THINGS THAT WERE MAGICAL THE FIRST TIME I DID THEM

SEEING THE MILKY WAY IN COSTA RICA

THE MOST SPIRITUAL EXPERIENCES I'VE HAD SO FAR

MY OUT-OF-BODY EXPERIENCE

TIMES I'VE EXPERIENCED SOMETHING
SUPERNATURAL OR INTUITIVE

ULURU-KATA TJUTA NATIONAL PARK, AUSTRALIA

SPIRITUAL PLACES

I'VE VISITED

HOPE TO VISIT

☐ ------------------------------------

☐ ------------------------------------

☐ ------------------------------------

☐ ------------------------------------

☐ ------------------------------------

☐ ------------------------------------

☐ ------------------------------------

☐ ------------------------------------

☐ ------------------------------------

☐ ------------------------------------

☐ ------------------------------------

☐ ------------------------------------

☐ ------------------------------------

☐ ------------------------------------

☐ ------------------------------------

☐ ------------------------------------

☐ ------------------------------------

☐ ------------------------------------

☐ ------------------------------------

GOSSIPING

NEGATIVE THINGS TO AVOID PARTICIPATING IN

LESS TV

RUTS AND ROUTINES

RUTS TO CHANGE

NEW ROUTINE IDEAS

ANNUAL MEMORIAL DINNER FOR THOSE WHO HAVE PASSED

TRADITIONS TO CREATE

CAT STEVENS, 'THE WIND'

SONGS THAT ARE MY ANTHEMS

THINGS I FORGIVE MYSELF FOR . . .

WRITE, DRAW SYMBOLS, OR COLLAGE HERE

THINGS I FORGIVE MYSELF FOR . . .

WRITE, DRAW SYMBOLS, OR COLLAGE HERE

PEOPLE I FORGIVE

WRITE, DRAW SYMBOLS, OR COLLAGE HERE

PEOPLE I FORGIVE

.

WRITE, DRAW SYMBOLS, OR COLLAGE HERE

LUCILLE BALL

THE MAN WHO KNITTED SWEATERS FOR
PENGUINS AFTER AN OIL SPILL

INSPIRING PEOPLE AND ORGANIZATIONS

MAHARISHI MAHESH YOGI

HEROES, GURUS, AND MENTORS THROUGHOUT MY LIFE

DESSERT POTLUCK WITH FRIENDS

HOW I'D SPEND MY LAST DAY ON EARTH

THE WHITE STAR LINE ORCHESTRA CONTINUED
PLAYING DURING THE SINKING OF THE *TITANIC*

STORIES THAT INSPIRE ME

OPRAH'S *SUPER SOUL SUNDAY*

FILMS AND TV SHOWS THAT INSPIRE ME

MAN'S SEARCH FOR MEANING BY VIKTOR FRANKL

BOOKS THAT INSPIRE ME

MARINA ABRAMOVIĆ

HAPPY: PARADES

SAD: LITTERING

THE BEAUTIFUL BALANCE OF HAPPINESS AND SADNESS

THINGS THAT MAKE ME HAPPY

THINGS THAT MAKE ME SAD

YOU, YOURSELF, AS MUCH AS ANYBODY IN
THE ENTIRE UNIVERSE, DESERVE YOUR LOVE
AND AFFECTION. —BUDDHISM

TEACHINGS I LOVE FROM VARIOUS RELIGIONS

TEACHING

RELIGION

VOTE

WAYS TO BE ENGAGED POLITICALLY

WITH RESPECT

HOW I WANT TO BE TREATED BY OTHERS

THE QUALITIES OF MY SPIRIT ANIMAL

ANIMAL

MY PERSONAL MANTRAS

PRACTICE HANDSTANDS AND REMEMBER
NOTHING IS PERMANENT

THINGS TO THINK AND DO WHEN I AM FEELING DOWN

TO THINK

TO DO

MY EDUCATION

GOOD CHOICES I'VE MADE

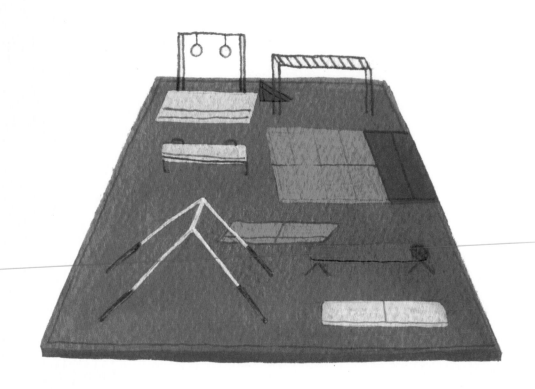

MISTAKE: QUITTING GYMNASTICS
LESSON: DON'T GIVE UP

WHAT I'VE LEARNED FROM MISTAKES

MISTAKE   LESSON

MY HIP-HOP CAREER

ACCOMPLISHMENTS AND PROUD FAILURES

ACCOMPLISHMENTS

PROUD FAILURES

AN UPGRADED AIRPLANE SEAT

GREET MOMENTS OF LUCK I'VE EXPERIENCED

THAT IT'S EMBARRASSING TO DANCE

WAYS OF THINKING I WANT TO UNLEARN

HOW HEALTHY I EAT

THINGS I CAN AND CAN'T CONTROL

CAN

CAN'T

I SOMETIMES HIDE CHOCOLATE BUNNIES FROM YOU

MY LITTLE CONFESSIONS

THAT I COULD PLAY THE PIANO

MEMORABLE DREAMS I'VE HAD

HARDEST: WITNESSING A CAR ACCIDENT

HAPPIEST AND HARDEST MOMENTS IN MY LIFE

HAPPIEST   HARDEST

A HOMEMADE PLUSH TOY FOR MY DOG

MEMORABLE GIFTS

I'VE GIVEN

HOPE TO GIVE

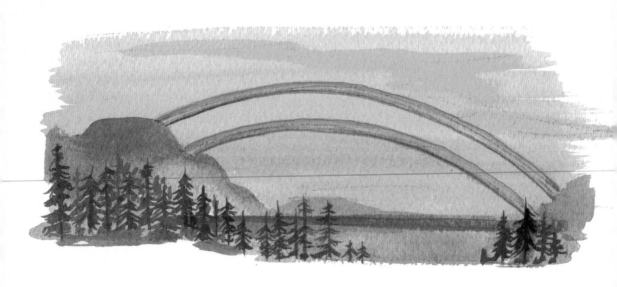

WHAT I AM GRATEFUL FOR

TO MY DAD FOR TEACHING ME HOW TO RIDE A BIKE

THANK-YOU SHOUT-OUTS

PERSON   THANK YOU FOR

_____   _____

_____   _____

_____   _____

_____   _____

_____   _____

_____   _____

_____   _____

_____   _____

_____   _____

_____   _____

_____   _____

_____   _____

_____   _____

_____   _____

_____   _____

_____   _____

_____   _____

_____   _____

"The world changes in direct proportion to the number of people willing to be honest about their lives."

-ARMISTEAD MAUPIN

INSPIRING QUOTES

MADE SOMEONE'S LIFE A LITTLE BETTER

THE LEGACY I WANT TO LEAVE BEHIND

LEARN TO PLAY THE BAGPIPES

LIFE IDEAS

- [ ] --
- [ ] --
- [ ] --
- [ ] --
- [ ] --
- [ ] --
- [ ] --
- [ ] --
- [ ] --
- [ ] --
- [ ] --
- [ ] --
- [ ] --
- [ ] --
- [ ] --
- [ ] --
- [ ] --
- [ ] --
- [ ] --
- [ ] --

TRAMPOLINING

IDEAS FOR NURTURING MYSELF

MIND   BODY

SOUL   CREATIVITY

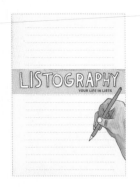
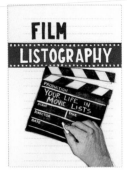
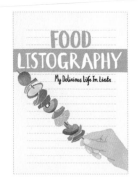
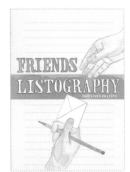

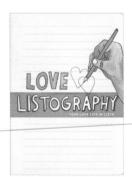

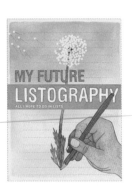

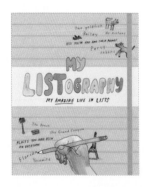
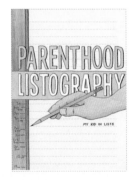
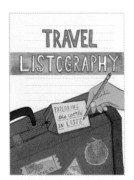